Challenging Puzzles
for Smart Kids

By Terry Stickels

imagine!
Publishing

Special thanks to Christy Davis, Elizabeth Anne Baker, Terry Baughan, Anthony Immanuvel, and Sam Bellotto Jr.

10 9 8 7 6 5 4 3

An Imagine Book
Published by Charlesbridge
85 Main Street
Watertown, MA 02472
617-926-0329
www.charlesbridge.com

Printed in China

ISBN 13: 978-1-936140-41-1

1. An anagram is a word whose letters can be rearranged to form a new word. One example is the word "read." Its letters can also make the word "dear." Which of the following is an anagram of the phrase "Angry me"?

a) a city
b) a country
c) an animal
d) a famous person

2. Can you give at least one example of where the number *eighty* appears before *seventy*? This is not a trick, nor does it have anything to do with mirror images or reversing letters or words.

3. What do you see in this picture?

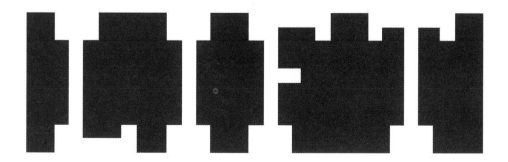

4. The puzzle below is called a *FILLAMINO*. The 6x6 square is divided into several different kinds of shapes. The numbers in the boxes tell you how many boxes will appear in each shape. No two shapes of the same size may touch each other directly, however their corners may touch.

Here's an example with its solution:

4	4			3	2
			2	4	4
4				4	4
		4	5	5	2
	1			5	5
5	4				5

4	4	3	3	2	2
4	1	3	2	4	4
4	5	1	2	4	4
5	5	4	5	5	2
5	1	4	5	5	2
5	4	4	1	5	1

Now you try. Can you figure out which shapes make up the square?

2	5	5	1	5	5
2	5	3	4	4	5
5	5	3	4	4	5
4	1	3	5	2	5
4	4	1	5	2	3
4	5	5	5	3	3

5. How many hours are there in 10,000 seconds?

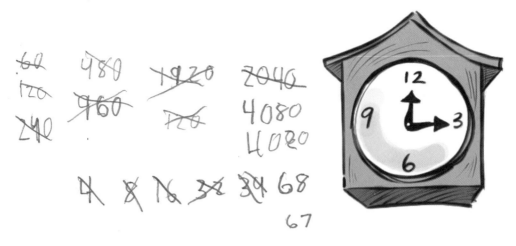

~~60~~   480   ~~1920~~   ~~2040~~
120   ~~960~~   4080
240   ~~720~~   4080

~~4~~ ~~8~~ ~~16~~ ~~32~~ ~~34~~ 68
67

6. What number comes next in the sequence?

3   6   9   15   24   39   63   _102_

7. The scrambled letters below represent a ten-letter word when unscrambled. See if you can unscramble the letters to come up with a common, everyday word.

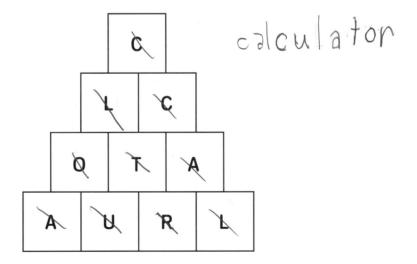

calculator

8. What one word can be placed before the four words below to make four new words?

_ _ _ _ script   _ _ _ _ card

_ _ _ _ age   P O S T man

Here's another one to try:

H a n d shake   H a n d some

H a n d writing   H a n d made

9. This type of puzzle is called a **STICKLINK**. The letters contain a hidden phrase. Here's how it works:

Step 1: To find the hidden phrase, start with the circled letter. The fill-in blanks at the bottom will also help.

Step 2: Draw a line from each correct letter to the next as you reveal the phrase.

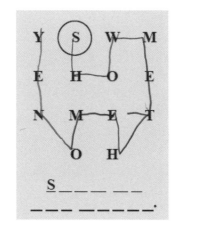

S _ _ _ _ _ _
_ _ _ _ _ _ _ .

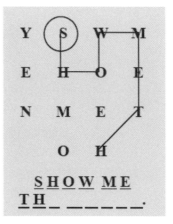

S H O W M E
T H _ _ _ _ _ _ .

Step 3: When done, each letter will be used only once and will be connected with a straight line.

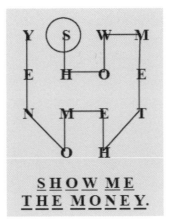

S H O W   M E
T H E   M O N E Y.

Now you try. HINT: Start with the circled letter. We've given you the quote's author.

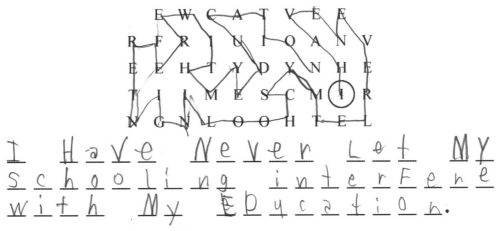

I Have Never Let My
Schooling interfere
with My Education.

Mark Twain—American Author

10. "Finer than a lark" is an anagram of one of the best-known singers in the world. Her music can be heard in every corner of the globe and is played in many languages. This singer is in the Rock 'n' Roll Hall of Fame and has a very "royal" nickname. Can you find the anagram?

11. This type of puzzle is called a *FRAME GAME*. Can you find the hidden word or phrase in the frame?

12. This type of puzzle is called a *WORDOKU*. Fill the grid with letters in such a way that all rows and columns have all letters once and only once. No two letters can be in the same row, column, or 3x3 box. One of the answers is the keyword: a nine-letter word that is correctly spelled out. It can be horizontal or vertical, and the keyword may be spelled backward. The keyword is LONGITUDE.

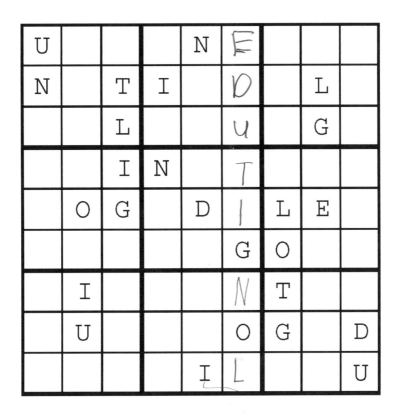

U				N	E			
N		T	I		D		L	
		L			U		G	
		I	N		T			
	O	G		D	I	L	E	
				G	O			
	I			N	T			
	U			O	G			D
			I	L				U

13. A year has one of them. A century has one of them. But a decade has two of them, as does an eternity. What is it they have?

E

14. Below is a puzzle called a **TRICKLEDOWN**. The goal of the puzzle is to arrive at the final word by changing one letter per line. Each letter change must result in a new word. Once a letter has been changed, it has to remain that way. There may be more than one answer, but the rules remain the same. See how quickly you can reach the bottom.

Here's an example with its solution:

M A L T	MALT
_____	MART
_____	CART
_____	CARD
C O R D	CORD

Now you try:

B L O C K

_____ Black

_____ Slack

_____ STack

_____ Stark

S T A R T

15. One of these words does not belong with the others. Which one and why?

magenta   amber   chartreuse   ridge   scarlet

16. This kind of puzzle is called a *TOWER SUDOKU*. Fill the grid with digits 1−4 in such a way that all rows and columns have all digits once and only once. The numbers outside specify how many towers can be seen from that position if the digits represent the height (number of floors) or towers. In other words, in the example below, look at the 1 on the outside bottom row of the grid in the answer section. This 1 means you can only see 1 tower looking up that column because the number 4 is the first tower, so it would block all the others. Look at the number 3 next to it. This means you will see 3 towers looking up that column: 1, 3, and 4.

Here's an example with its solution:

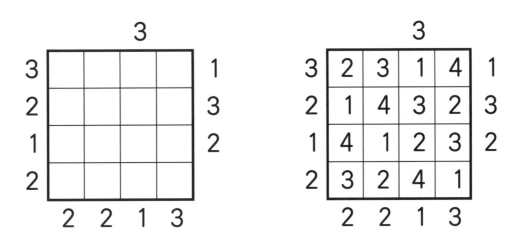

Now you try:

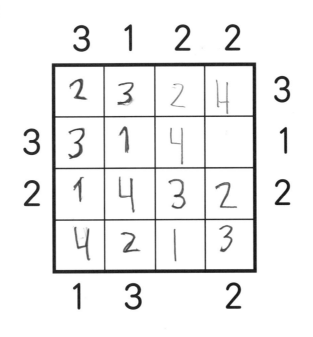

17. This kind of puzzle is called a **HEXAGONY**. Fit the hexagonal shapes into each honeycomb in such a way that all neighboring triangles of adjacent hexagons have the same digits. You cannot rotate the hexagons.

Here's an example with its solution:

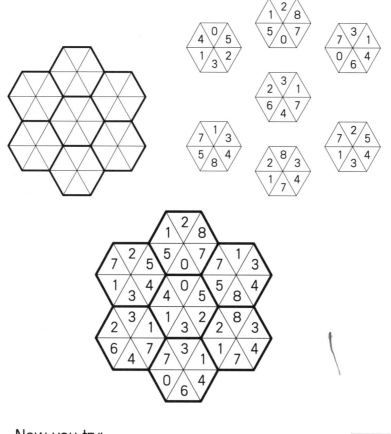

Now you try:

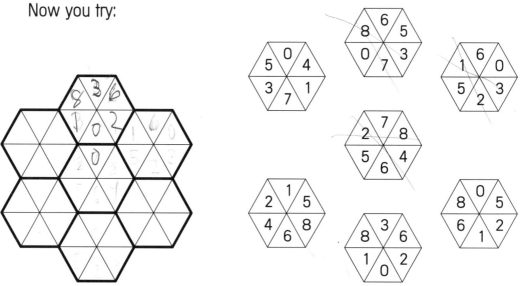

18. If today is Thursday, what is three days before the day after tomorrow?

wehnsday

19. Two of the following statements are false. Knowing that, can you find the correct name of each person?

1. Amelia's last name is Juarez. √
2. Sandra's last name is Clark. ✗
3. Amelia's last name is Clark. ✗

20. Comparing scores of different ball games has always been a fun pastime and people have been doing it for many years. Below are the scores of three fictitious ball games. Based on the information you have, compare the scores and figure out who would win a game if Michigan were to play Baylor.

Michigan	27	Nebraska	21
Nebraska	14	Oklahoma	13
Oklahoma	10	Baylor	3

21. This type of puzzle is called a **SQUEEZER**. To solve the puzzle, find the word that fits between the two given words on each line, making two new words, one from the back and one from the front. The number of spaces represents the number of letters in the **SQUEEZER** word.

Example: FIRE _ _ _ _ WORK

FIRE w o o d WORK

Now you try:

1. TRAP _ _ _ _ KNOB

2. MASTER _ _ _ _ LESS

3. PLAY _ _ _ _ _ _ HOG

22. If there are 12 dibs in a dreb, 10 drebs in a drope, and 3 dropes in a dubisk, how many dibs are in three dubisks?

23. Marley the Mouse is about to enter a maze where each block has a rule on how to proceed. The left to right directions are from Marley's point of view, while the north, south, east, and west directions are indicated by the map legend. If the directions tell him to leave a block in a certain direction, he will depart the block in the middle. That is, if he has to turn, he turns in the middle of the block to leave.

What is the letter of the block where Marley will exit the maze?

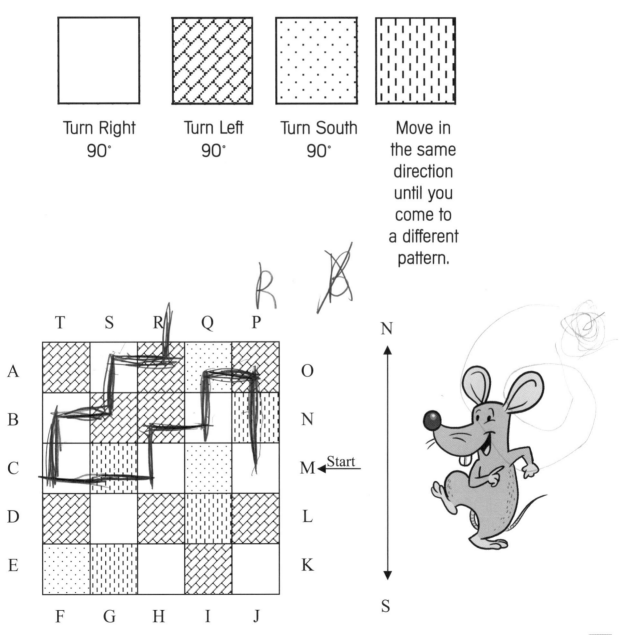

Turn Right 90°

Turn Left 90°

Turn South 90°

Move in the same direction until you come to a different pattern.

24. Here's a fun crossword puzzle for you to try.

(1 across filled in: f r e s h)

ACROSS

1 Just picked
5 School group
8 Whole-wheat or white
9 Cruel
10 Record
12 Comic strip
15 Individual
17 Backyard wear
18 *Shrek* princess
19 Storyline
20 Yogi Bear's nemesis
22 Something to skip
23 Tournament
25 Make money
26 School subject
28 Pester
29 Museum hangings
30 In the neighborhood
31 In the form of Humpty-Dumpty

DOWN

1 Drastic food shortage
2 Ice cream parlor treat
3 TV's "Star_____"
4 Powder-puff powder
6 Santa checks it twice
7 Poem with 14 lines
11 Word ending
13 Penguins' home ice
14 In hock
15 At the mall, perhaps
16 Typical
19 How some mail is marked
21 Shot up like a spacecraft
23 Make
24 Garage job
25 Even-steven
26 Emulate the Jonas Brothers
27 React to a mosquito bite

25. a) What would you call your mother-in-law's only child's father-in-law?

   b) If a gardener has 1,000 plants and all but 999 die, how many plants are left?

   c) There are two cats in front of a cat and two cats behind a cat . . . and one cat in the middle.
   What is the minimum number of cats?

26. Here are four words that you may find hard to spell. They are turned upside down so you won't be inclined to sneak a peek. Try to spell these with friends and family. It can be lots of fun.

Moratorium

uʍǝlos   uƃᴉsuǝ   ɯnᴉɹoʇɐɹoɯ   ɯɹǝpʎɥɔɐd

27. This kind of puzzle is called a **STICKDOKU**. Stickdoku (also known as Sudoku) is a number puzzle with a 9x9 grid and numbers known as clues printed in squares.

The goal is to complete the grid in such a way that all rows, columns, and highlighted 3x3 squares contain the digits 1–9 once and only once.

Can you fill in the empty squares?

			1	3				
		7		9	8	4	6	
	7	2				1		
3					9		4	
2	6						1	
	2			7	3			
7	1	5	6		2			
		4	8					

28. Find the pattern that the letters in the figures below follow to spell out a sentence. The blanks beneath the figures represent the number of letters in each word of the sentence. See how long it takes you to find the sentence.

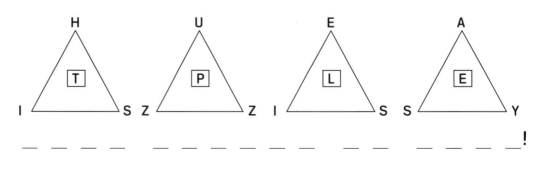

_ !

29. The three items in each list below have one thing in common. Can you find it? Here's an example:

1) a sewing needle
2) a hurricane
3) Mississippi

Answer: All have eyes.

Now you try:

a) 1) the constellation Orion
   2) a conveyor
   3) a karate expert

b) 1) sheet music
   2) a front door
   3) a piano

c) 1) a living human
   2) an artichoke
   3) a deck of playing cards

d) 1) a squirrel
   2) a baseball
   3) a spoon

e) 1) a fish
   2) a butcher shop
   3) musical instrument practice

30. Can you find the missing number in the sequence?

7   66   555   4444   33333   **?**   1111111

31. A strange, distant land has a number system that uses the same numbers we do, but the numbers have different values. Their values are consistent and it's possible to convert their numbers to ours. For example, their number 2 is equal to our number 7. Likewise, their number 4 is equal to our 14, and their number 8 is equal to our 28.

Can you figure out what their number 10 is equal to in our number system? What is their number 3 equal to?

32. This kind of puzzle is called an **ARITHMETIC SQUARE**. Fill in the white blanks with numbers and one of the three operations: +, - , or x. (There is no division in this puzzle.) The numbers outside the grid tell you the solution to the arithmetic problem. Remember, multiplication comes before addition and subtraction in the order of operations.

Here's an example with its solution:

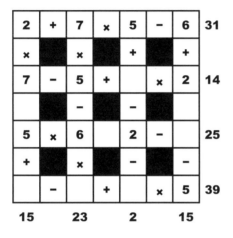 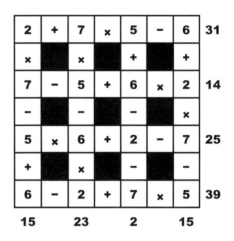

Now you try:

2	**+**	**8**	**+**	**7**	**x**	**5**	**45**
+		**+**				**x**	
7	**x**	**5**		**2**	**x**	**8**	**19**
+		**x**		**−**		**+**	
5	**x**	**2**		**1**	**+**		**16**
x		**−**		**x**		**−**	
8	**x**		**−**	**5**		**2**	**53**

49   **11**   **4**   **45**

33. This kind of puzzle is called a *FUTOSHIKI*. Place digits 1–5 in the grid. Each row and column should have all digits once and only once. The ❭ (greater than) and ❬ (lesser than) symbols between cells indicate which cell has a larger number.

Here's an example with its solution:

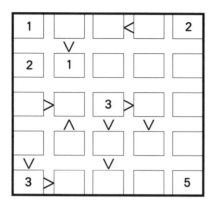 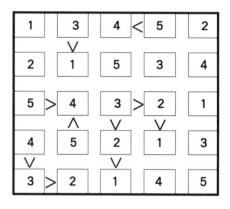

Now you try:

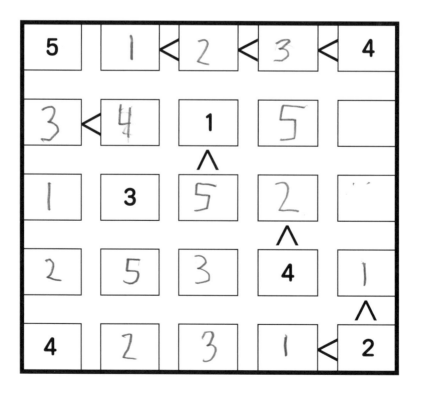

34. How many individual cubes are in the stack below? All rows and columns run to completion unless you actually see them end. The bottom row in the middle of the stack has no cubes in it.

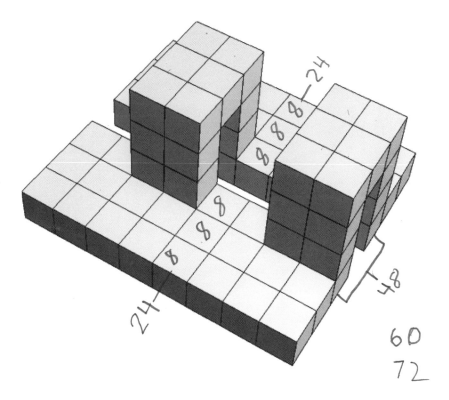

35. Below is a school bus that is moving forward. Can you tell which way it's moving—left or right? There is a logical way to figure this out.

36. Can you figure out where each unique domino piece is placed in this puzzle? To help you, a set of unique domino pieces is given. Just like a domino, each piece consists of two numbers. They may be placed forward, backward, or even vertically in the grid, just not diagonally.

Here's an example:

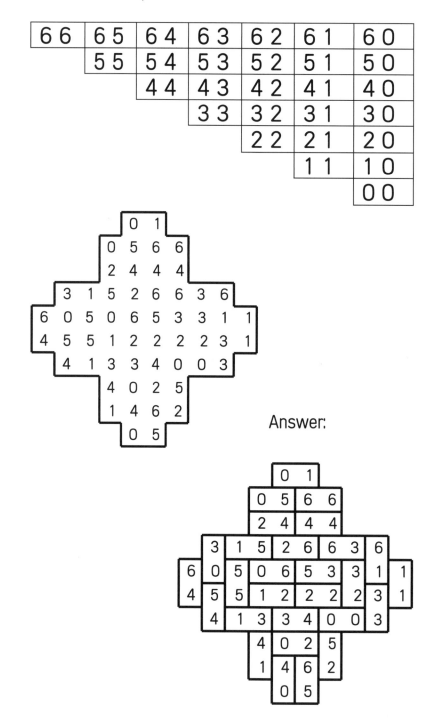

Answer:

Now you try:

6 6	6 5	6 4	6 3	6 2	6 1	6 0
	5 5	5 4	5 3	5 2	5 1	5 0
		4 4	4 3	4 2	4 1	4 0
			3 3	3 2	3 1	3 0
				2 2	2 1	2 0
					1 1	1 0
						0 0

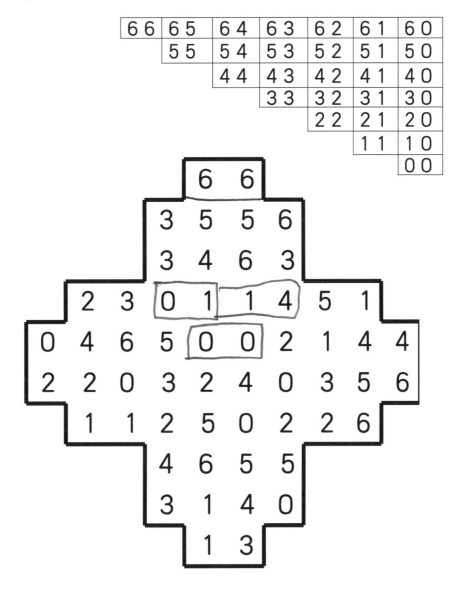

```
            6  6
      3  5  5  6
      3  4  6  3
2  3  0  1  1  4  5  1
0  4  6  5  0  0  2  1  4  4
2  2  0  3  2  4  0  3  5  6
1  1  2  5  0  2  2  6
      4  6  5  5
      3  1  4  0
         1  3
```

37. Which two shapes below can be placed together to make the larger shape?

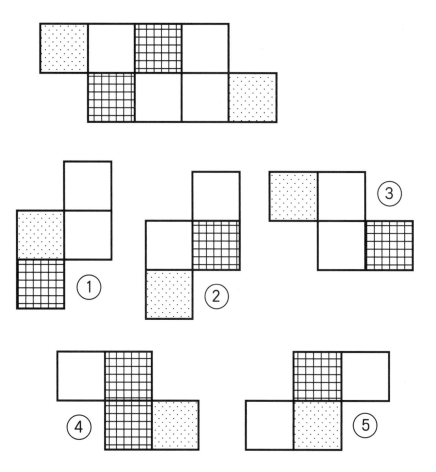

38. This type of puzzle is called a **CRYPTOGRAM**. In this cryptogram, you must determine which symbol represents the appropriate letter of the alphabet to decode the message. Here is a hint to get you started. The first letter is I, ε equals E, and ψ equals Y.

Ιτ'σ αμαζινγ τηατ τηε αμουντ οφ νεωσ τηατ

ηαππενσ ιν τηε ωορλδ εϖερψ δαψ αλωαψσ φυστ

εξαχτλψ φιτσ τηε νεωσπαπερ.—ϑερρψ Σεινφελδ

39. One of these four figures does not belong with the other figures based on a simple, straightforward design feature. Which is the odd one out?

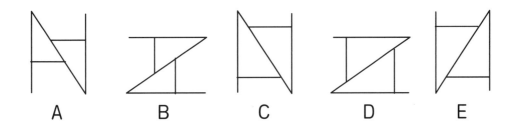

A   B   C   D   E

40. Find the hidden word or phrase in the **FRAME GAME** below:

41. Three of the numbers below are divisible by 9 with no remainder. There is a quick way to find out which three, if you know some simple rules of division. Which three?

1,000   3,333   575

369   7,002   666,666

42. This kind of puzzle is called a *HITORI*. Shade the numbers in such a way that:

1. The unshaded numbers do not have any repetition of that number in the row or column.
2. Shaded numbers are not adjacent, either horizontally or vertically, but can touch diagonally.
3. The unshaded numbers create a single shape of horizontally and vertically connected cells that run throughout the grid.

Here's an example with its solution:

5	3	5	1	4	2
1	5	2	2	3	5
2	2	4	3	5	3
3	2	3	4	3	5
5	5	1	3	2	4
3	4	2	4	1	2

5	3	5	1	4	2
1	5	2	2	3	5
2	2	4	3	5	3
3	2	3	4	3	5
5	5	1	3	2	4
3	4	2	4	1	2

Now you try:

3	2	2	3	1	1
4	3	2	1	3	5
2	3	3	4	5	1
4	4	5	3	3	5
3	1	2	5	2	4
4	5	1	5	4	5

43. There is an old puzzle that asks if you can arrange six toothpicks into four equilateral triangles.

The usual solution given is a three-dimensional figure called a *tetrahedron*.

Here's a new version of the puzzle. Can you take six toothpicks and make eight equilateral triangles?

44. The numbers 1−16 can be placed in the magic square so that each of the rows, columns, and diagonals has the same sum. Can you fill in the remaining numbers?

	13	12	7
11	8		14
5		15	
16	3		

45. The faces of ten identical cubes are fused together as seen below. (There is one hidden cube between to 2, 4, and 8. It is cube number 10.)

How many total faces are fused together?

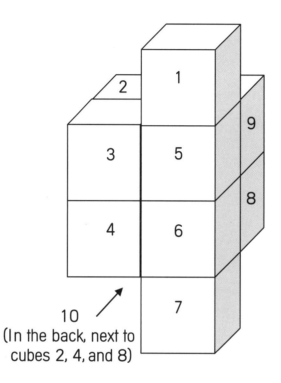

10
(In the back, next to cubes 2, 4, and 8)

46. Five of these six words below share a common feature. Which word is the odd one out? HINT: View these words from different perspectives.

Rotator   Noon

Civic   Redder

Pools   Level

47. Below are three views of the same cube.

If you were to unfold the cube and lay it flat on a table, how would the remaining faces appear on the layout below?

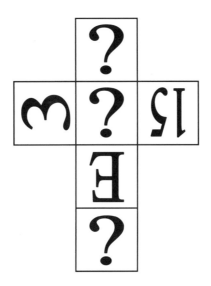

48. Which line is longer, from A to B or from B to C?

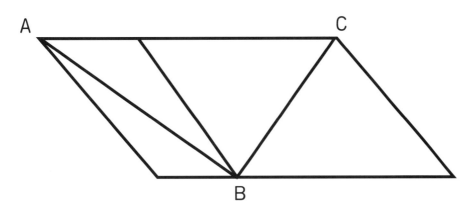

49. This puzzle doesn't have a name, but it's been around for fifty years and is great fun to solve. The abbreviations below stand for a common phrase, idiom, book, song title, game, etc. Here's an example of how it works:

1) 16 = O in a P
2) 9 = I in a B G
3) 8 = P of S in the E L

Answers:
1) 16 ounces in a pound
2) 9 innings in a baseball game
3) 8 parts of speech in the English language

Now you try:

1)   26 = L of the A
2)   1001 = A N
3)   7 = W of the W
4)   12 = S of the Z
5)   54 = C in a D (with the J)
6)   9 = P in the S S
7)   88 = P K
8)   13 = S on the A F
9)   32 = D F at which W F
10) 18 = H on a G C
11) 90 = D in a R A

12) 200 = D for P G in M
13) 8 = S on a S S
14) 3 = B M (S H T R)
15) 4 = Q in a G
16) 24 = H in a D
17) 1 = W on a U
18) 5 = D in a Z C
19) 57 = H V
20) 11 = P on a F T
21) 29 = D in F in a L Y
22) 64 = S on a C

50. Here is another *WORDOKU*. The keyword is KEYBOARDS.

					E		B	
Y			D		R			
						R	O	Y
O			E	S			Y	
				A				
	D			K	O			A
A	E	B						
			K		A			D
	R		O					

51. The numbers in each of the circles below have a relationship that is the same across each circle. That relationship determines the bottom number in each circle. What's the missing number in the last circle?

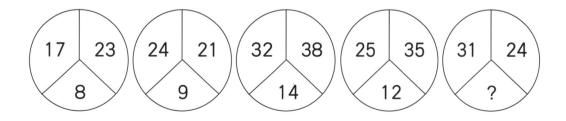

52. See how long it takes you to weave your way through this maze.

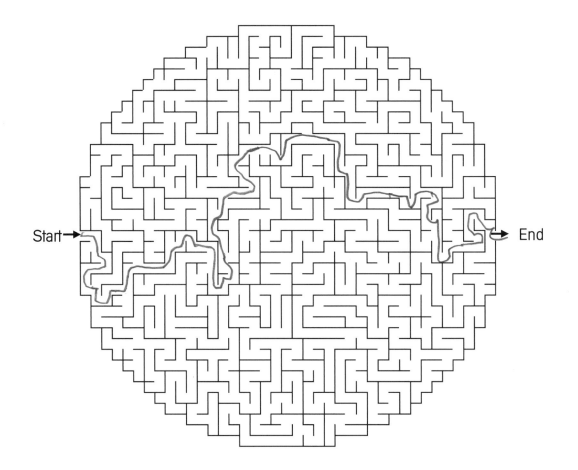

Start→   End

53. The number in the middle of each grid is a result of operations performed on the other four numbers. The operations are the same for each box. What number goes in the last box?

5		12
	10	
19		4

13		7
	13	
27		5

30		2
	15	
11		17

25		35
	18	
9		3

6		4
	?	
21		1

54. Each block below is the same size and each block has six faces. How many other blocks does the face or side of each block touch? Blocks that connect at the edges or corners don't count.

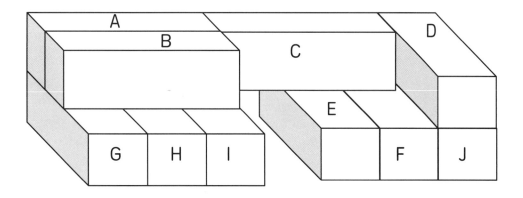

55. Aman, Betsy, and Colin compared the amount of change each had after lunch at school. Aman and Betsy had $0.12 together, Betsy and Colin had $0.18 together, and Aman and Colin had $0.10 together. Who had the least amount of money and how much was it?

56. There is a well-known puzzle that asks you to move two toothpicks to create two squares, using only the eight toothpicks in the configuration below.

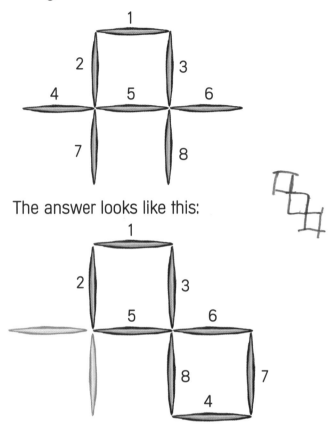

The answer looks like this:

See if you can take these same eight toothpicks and create three squares. The squares can be of any size and you can move as many toothpicks as you choose.

57. Here is another **CRYPTOGRAM**. See how fast you can determine which symbol represents the correct letter of the alphabet and decode the message. Hint: ♋ is equal to A, ♏ is equal to E, ♑ is equal to G, ☹ is equal to L, and ■ is equal to N.

♨♏♑♓■ ♋♦ ♦♒♏ ♌♏♑♓■■♓■♑ ♋■♎ ♑♉ ♉■
♦♓●● ♉♉♦ ♑♉♉♏ ♦♉ ♦♒♏ ♏■♎; ♦♒♏■ ♦♦♉♉.

−☹♏♦♓♦ ♨♋♉♉♉●●

58. How many different words can you make from the word "weights?" You may be surprised how many there are. You can make up your own rules as to which words qualify. One of the most common ways is to use common words found in a dictionary. That's the method we used here to come up with our answers. We'll give you a list of answers in the answer section . . . but our list does not mean there are no more words.
See if you can add to what we have. NOTE: Since each of the seven different letters in "weights" appears only once, our answers only use each letter once.

59. Before your digital clock is plugged in and lighted, the segments for its numbers are laid out like this (this is a digital clock that is a twelve-hour clock, not a twenty-four-hour clock).

Depending upon the time, the appropriate segments are lit up for you to see the time.

1) What time uses the fewest number of segments?

2) What time is it when the greatest number of segments are on?

60. Here is another Marley the Mouse puzzle.

Marley enters the maze and moves from left to right. The left to right directions are from his point of view, while the north, south, east, and west directions are indicated by the map legend. If the directions tell him to leave a block in a certain direction, he will depart the block in the middle. That is, if he has to turn, he turns in the middle of the block to leave.

What is the letter or number of the block where Marley will exit?

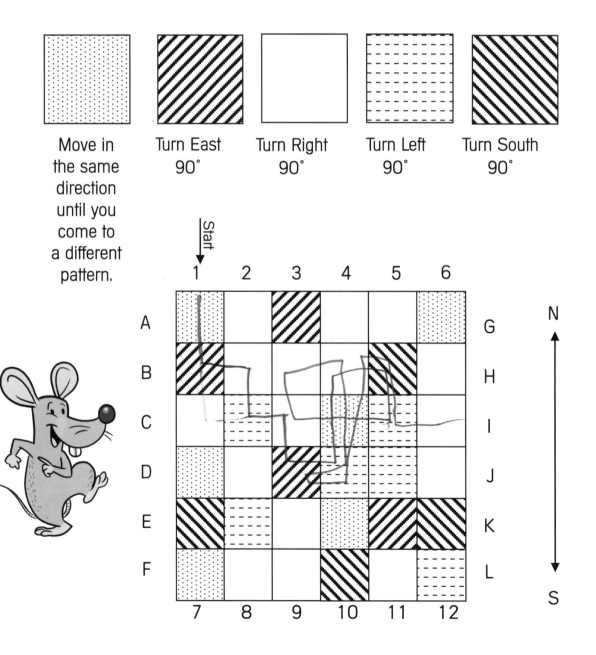

| Move in the same direction until you come to a different pattern. | Turn East 90° | Turn Right 90° | Turn Left 90° | Turn South 90° |

61. Are the lines in the picture below slanted at 20 degrees, 30 degrees, or are they parallel?

62. Here is another **STICKLINK** for you. See if you can find the hidden phrase.

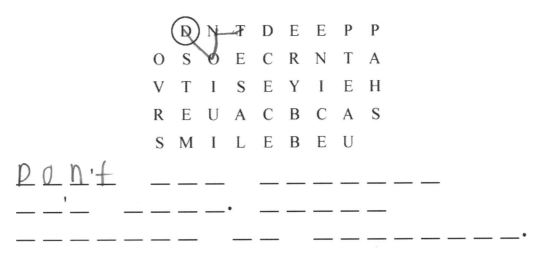

Dr. Seuss—Children's Author

63. Here is another *HEXAGONY* puzzle. Fit the hexagonal shapes into each honeycomb in such a way that all neighboring triangles of adjacent hexagons have the same digits. Remember, you cannot rotate the hexagons.

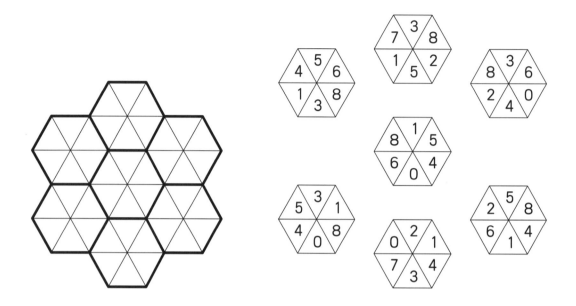

64. See if you can find the clue in 1) and 2) that will help you find the missing word.

1) bookkeeper   perish   skittish
2) calendar   darted   prompted
3) emblem   **(?)**   coupons

65. Find the hidden word or phrase in the **FRAME GAME** below.

66. There are two states in the United States that each have eight different states touching them. They also touch each other. One of the states is Missouri. What is the other state, and can you name the states adjacent to Missouri and the other state?

67. Can you figure out where each unique domino piece is placed in this puzzle? To help you, a set of unique domino pieces is given. Just like a domino, each piece consists of two numbers. They may be placed forward, backward, or even horizontally in the grid, just not diagonally.

6 6	6 5	6 4	6 3	6 2	6 1	6 0
	5 5	5 4	5 3	5 2	5 1	5 0
		4 4	4 3	4 2	4 1	4 0
			3 3	3 2	3 1	3 0
				2 2	2 1	2 0
					1 1	1 0
						0 0

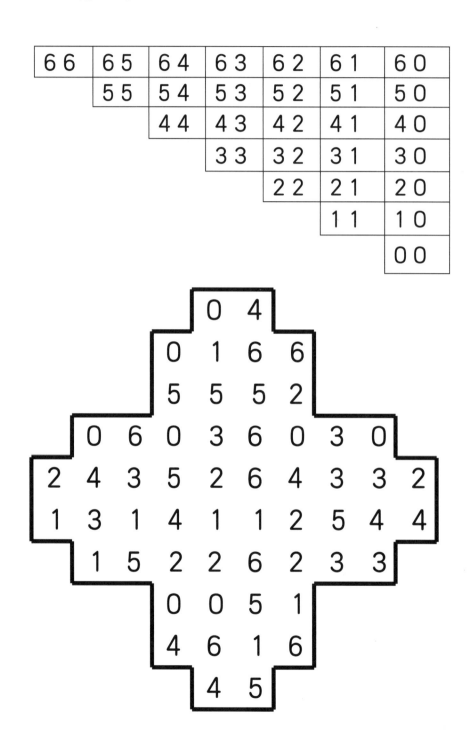

68. Are there more than twenty-five curved lines in this picture?

69. Arm, ear, eye, gum, hip, jaw, leg, lip, rib, toe . . . these are the ten commonly known parts of the human body spelled with only three letters. How many parts of the human body can you name that are spelled with only four letters? You can use plurals. This is a fun puzzle to do with your family or friends to see who can find the most in the quickest amount of time.

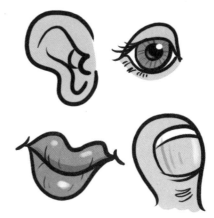

70. Here is another *STICKDOKU*. Complete the grid in such a way that all rows, columns, and highlighted 3x3 squares contain the digits 1–9 once and only once.

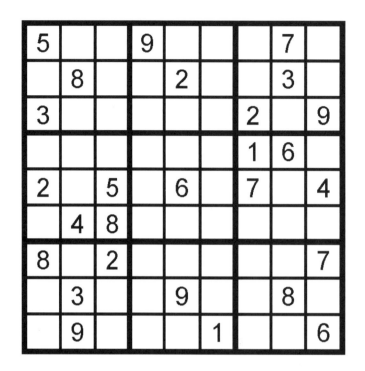

71. Molly was telling her friend that her grandmother, Sue, is only eight years older than her mother, Barbara. Her friend said, "That can't possibly be." Molly replied, "It's true, and I can explain it."

How is this possible?

72. There is an old puzzle where you are asked to connect as many dots as possible in a grid of 3x3 . . . without lifting your pencil or crossing any lines you may have already drawn. All lines must be straight and no diagonals are allowed. The usual answer given has ten connections and looks like this:

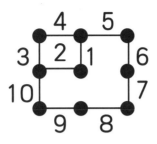

Now see how many dots you can connect in a 4x4 grid. Can you get at least eighteen or nineteen connections?

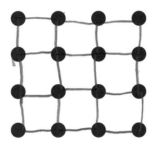

73. How many numbers between 1 and 100 can divide into 107 and leave a remainder of 4?

74. Here is another *TOWER SUDOKU*. Fill the grid with digits 1−4 in such a way that all rows and columns have all digits once and only once. The numbers outside specify how many towers can be seen from that position if the digits represent the height (number of floors) or towers.

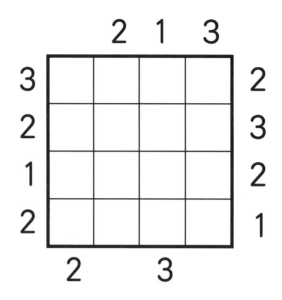

75. Look at the middle circles in each of the two pictures below. Which is bigger, the one on the left . . . or the one on the right?

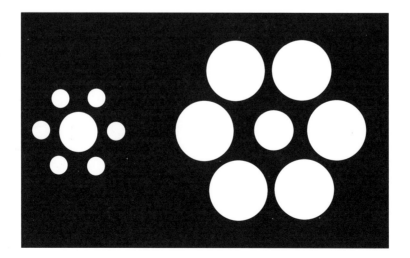

76. Here is another *FUTOSHIKI*. Place digits 1−5 in the grid. Each row and column should have all digits once and only once. The 〉 (greater than) and 〈 (lesser than) symbols between cells indicate which cell has a larger number.

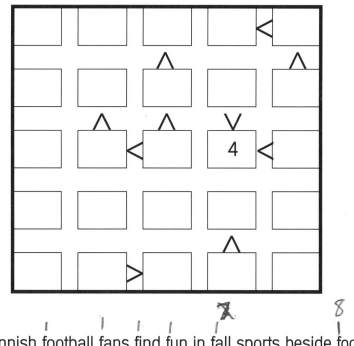

77. Friendly Finnish football fans find fun in fall sports beside football. For example, of all the sports there are outside, including fishing on frosty mornings, they enjoy fencing even though it is an off season activity and indoors. Fun for all.

How many times does the letter *F* appear in the above paragraph?

78. Find the hidden word or phrase in this *FRAME GAME*:

79. Can you create the following figure without lifting your pencil, retracing, or crossing another line? You can create the lines by going from corner to corner or in segments.

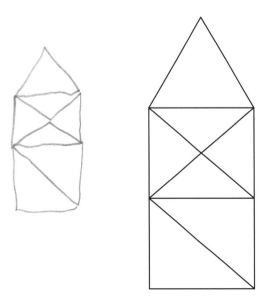

80. Here is another *FUTOSHIKI*. Place digits 1–5 in the grid. Each row and column should have all digits once and only once. The > (greater than) and < (lesser than) symbols between cells indicate which cell has a larger number.

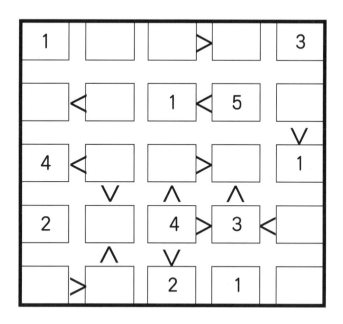

81. What letter is to the right of the letter that is two letters below the letter three letters to the right of the letter above the letter K?

A	B	C	D	E
F	G	H	I	J
K	L	M	N	O
P	Q	R	S	T
U	V	W	X	Y

82. There are fifteen words hidden in the grid below. The words can go horizontally, vertically, or diagonally, and may run forward or backward. Can you find them all?

Adjectives

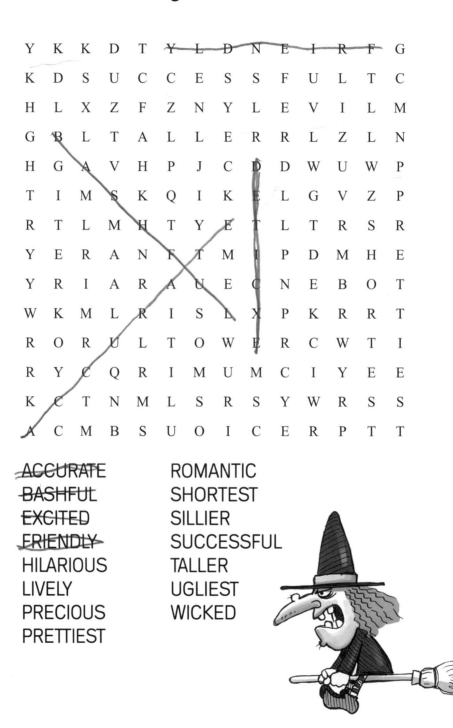

```
Y  K  K  D  T  Y  L  D  N  E  I  R  F  G
K  D  S  U  C  C  E  S  S  F  U  L  T  C
H  L  X  Z  F  Z  N  Y  L  E  V  I  L  M
G  B  L  T  A  L  L  E  R  R  L  Z  L  N
H  G  A  V  H  P  J  C  D  D  W  U  W  P
T  I  M  S  K  Q  I  K  E  L  G  V  Z  P
R  T  L  M  H  T  Y  E  T  L  T  R  S  R
Y  E  R  A  N  F  T  M  I  P  D  M  H  E
Y  R  I  A  R  A  U  E  C  N  E  B  O  T
W  K  M  L  R  I  S  L  X  P  K  R  R  T
R  O  R  U  L  T  O  W  E  R  C  W  T  I
R  Y  C  Q  R  I  M  U  M  C  I  Y  E  E
K  C  T  N  M  L  S  R  S  Y  W  R  S  S
A  C  M  B  S  U  O  I  C  E  R  P  T  T
```

ACCURATE   ROMANTIC
BASHFUL   SHORTEST
EXCITED   SILLIER
FRIENDLY   SUCCESSFUL
HILARIOUS   TALLER
LIVELY   UGLIEST
PRECIOUS   WICKED
PRETTIEST

83. You have been selected for a game show because they found out how smart you really are. You can solve almost any logic problem. You have the chance to win $1,000,000 if you can solve a logic puzzle in thirty seconds on national TV. You will be given four clues, three of which are false. Are you ready?

1) Pam: Steve or Regina has the check for $1,000,000.

2) Steve: Pam or Shawna has the $1,000,000 check.

3) Regina: I have it.

4) Shawna: I don't have it.

Who has it?

84. Believe it or not, a perfectly formed five-point star is hidden somewhere in the quilt below. See how long it takes you to find it.

85. Here is another *HITORI*. Shade the numbers in such a way, that:

1. The unshaded numbers do not have any repetition of that number in the row or column.
2. Shaded numbers are not adjacent, either horizontally or vertically, but can touch diagonally.
3. The unshaded numbers create a single shape of horizontally and vertically connected cells that run throughout the grid.

1	2	5	5	1	1
3	5	1	5	4	2
2	1	3	4	5	1
1	5	4	5	2	5
4	5	3	3	1	1
1	4	2	1	3	1

86. This puzzle was given to me by one of the best puzzle writers of all time: Martin Gardner. This was his favorite puzzle and he was delighted to show it over and over again.

Take five toothpicks and form the figure of a giraffe, as is shown in the diagram below. Now, move just one toothpick so that the shape of the giraffe remains the same, but the giraffe is rotated or reflected.

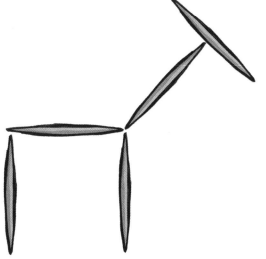

87. Find the hidden word or phrase in the **FRAME GAME** below:

88. Here is another *TOWER SUDOKU*. Fill the grid with digits 1–4 in such a way that all rows and columns have all digits once and only once. The numbers outside specify how many towers can be seen from that position if the digits represent the height (number of floors) of towers.

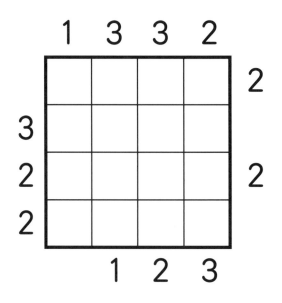

89. Here is another *HEXAGONY* puzzle. Fit the hexagonal shapes into each honeycomb in such a way that all neighboring triangles of adjacent hexagons have the same digits. Remember, you cannot rotate the hexagons.

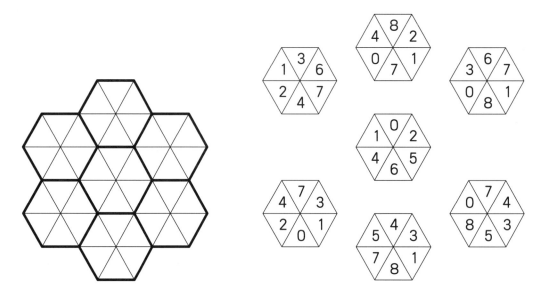

90. See how long it takes you to weave your way through this maze.

Start

End

Answers:

1. b) a country
The phrase "Angry me" is an anagram of "Germany."

2. The dictionary

3. The word "LIFT" is spelled out in white letters.

4.

2	5	5	1	5	5
2	5	3	4	4	5
5	5	3	4	4	5
4	1	3	5	2	5
4	4	1	5	2	3
4	5	5	5	3	3

5. 2.78 hours
Divide 10,000 by 60 to get the number of minutes.
10,000/60 = 166.67 minutes. Now, divide by 60 again to get the number of hours. 166.67/60 = 2.78 hours.

6. 102
Starting with the number 9, each number is the sum of the two preceding numbers.

7. Calculator

8. Post
The new words become postscript, postcard, postage, and postman.

Hand
The new words become handshake, handsome, handwriting, and handmade.

9.

I HAVE NEVER LET MY
SCHOOLING INTERFERE
WITH MY EDUCATION.

Mark Twain—American Author

10. "Finer than a lark" is an anagram for Aretha Franklin, the "Queen of Soul."

11. Win With Ease

12.

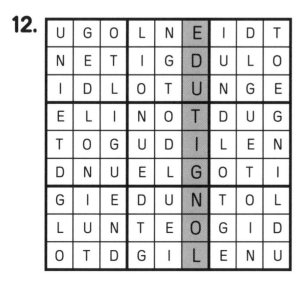

13. They have the letter *e* that many times in the spelling of their respective names.

14. Here is one way to solve the *TRICKLEDOWN*:

BLOCK
BLACK
SLACK
STACK
STARK
START

15. Ridge
The other words are all colors.

16.

	3	1	2	2	
	2	4	3	1	3
3	1	3	2	4	1
2	3	1	4	2	2
	4	2	1	3	
	1	3		2	

17.

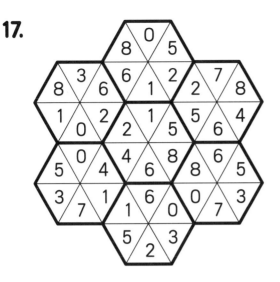

18. Wednesday

The day after tomorrow is Saturday. Three days before that would be Friday (the first day), Thursday (the second day) and Wednesday, the answer.

19. Sandra's last name is Juarez and Amelia's last name is Clark. Look at statements 1 and 3. One of those two statements must be wrong. Amelia cannot be both Clark and Juarez. Since one of those is wrong, the other must be right. That means statement 2 must be wrong. (Remember, only one of the three statements is true.) So Sandra's name must be Sandra Juarez and Amelia's name must be Amelia Clark.

20. Michigan

Michigan beat Nebraska by 6 points and Nebraska beat Oklahoma by 1, so Michigan would have beaten Oklahoma by 7, had they played. Oklahoma beat Baylor by 7, so this means Michigan would have beaten Baylor by 7+7, or 14 points.

21. 1. Door
2. Mind
3. Ground

22. 1,080 dibs
If there are 12 dibs in a dreb, then there are 120 dibs in a drope (12 dibs times 10 drebs) and 360 dibs in a dubisk (3 dropes times 120 = 360) . . . so, there are 360 dibs in a dubisk, but we have three dubisks. 3 times 360 = 1,080 dibs.

23. R

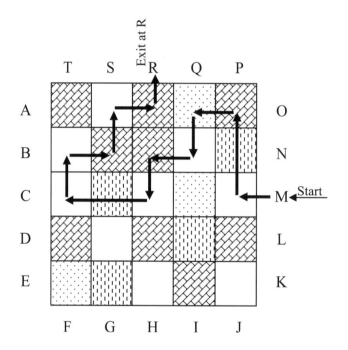

24.

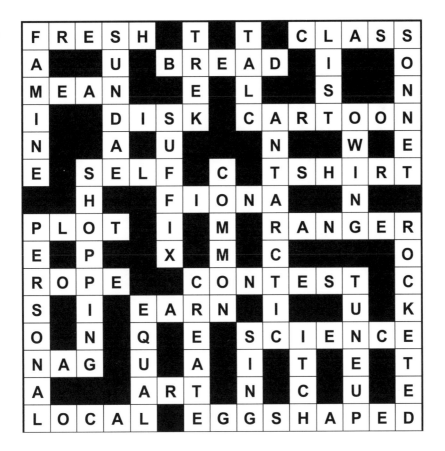

25. a) You call him dad!
b) 999 plants.
c) There are 3 cats.

26. Solemn
Ensign
Moratorium
Pachyderm

27.

5	6	4	8	1	3	2	7	9
1	3	2	7	5	9	8	4	6
9	8	7	2	6	4	5	1	3
3	7	1	5	2	6	9	8	4
8	4	9	3	7	1	6	5	2
2	5	6	9	4	8	7	3	1
4	2	8	1	9	7	3	6	5
7	1	5	6	3	2	4	9	8
6	9	3	4	8	5	1	2	7

28. This puzzle is easy!
Start with the letter T in the middle of the first figure.
Then move to the top of the first figure and continue
counterclockwise. Follow the same pattern with each
triangle.

29. a) All have belts.
b) All have keys.
c) All have hearts.
d) All have double letters in them.
e) All have scales.

30. 222222
The numeral used goes down by one each time, but an
additional digit is added. One seven, two sixes, three fives,
and so on.

31. Their number 10 is equal to our number 35. There are several ways to approach this. One way is to see that since their number 2 is equal to our number 7, we can multiply the 2 by 5 to get 10 . . . and also multiply 7 by 5 to get 35.

You can also solve this by setting up a proportion where 2 is to 7 as 10 is to x: $\frac{2}{7} = \frac{10}{x}$. Cross multiply and you get $2x = 70$ $x = 35$. Using this proportion also works for their number 3: $\frac{2}{7} = \frac{3}{x}$; $2x = 21$; $x = 10.5$. So, their number 3 is equal to our 10.5.

32.

2	+	8	+	7	×	5	45
+		+		+		×	
7	×	5	–	2	×	8	19
+		×		–		+	
5	×	2	–	1	+	7	16
×		–		×		–	
8	×	7	–	5	+	2	53
49		11		4		45	

33.

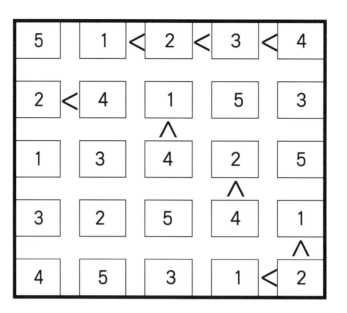

34. 76 cubes

35. The bus is moving left. You can tell because you can't see the door that lets you in and out of the bus.

36.

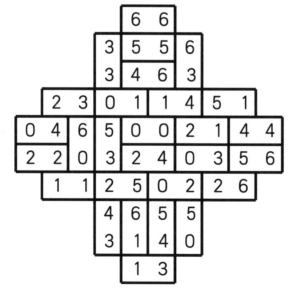

37. Shapes 2 and 3

38. It's amazing that the amount of news that happens in the world every day always just exactly fits the newspaper.—Jerry Seinfeld

39. E
All the other shapes have a large Z shape in them. E has a S (backward Z).

40. Crossing Guards

41. 369; 7,002; and 666,666
A number is divisible by 9 if you can divide the sum of the digits by 9.

42.

3	2	2	3	1	1
4	3	2	1	3	5
2	3	3	4	5	1
4	4	5	3	3	5
3	1	2	5	2	4
4	5	1	5	4	5

43.

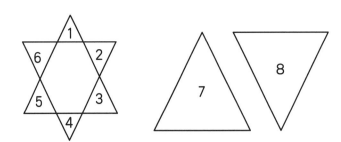

Six equilateral triangles of the same size and two other larger triangles, which are the same size.

44.

2	13	12	7
11	8	1	14
5	10	15	4
16	3	6	9

Look at the row beginning with 11. 11+8+14 = 33. You still need one more number, so each row, column, and diagonal will have a sum greater than 33.

Now look at the column beginning with 13. 13+8+3 = 24. Therefore, the only missing number in this column has to be greater than 9 (24+9 = 33). We've already used 11, 12, 13, 14, 15, and 16, so the only number left greater than 9 is 10. Now that you know each row, column, and diagonal totals 34, it's easy to fill in the rest.

45. 28

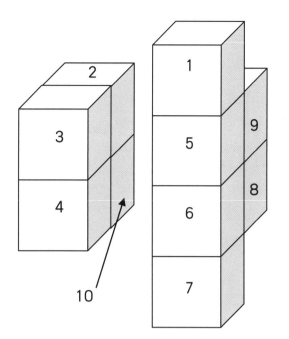

Face 1 = 1 (1-5)
Face 2 = 3 (2-3; 2-10; 2-9)
Face 3 = 3 (3-2; 3-4; 3-5)
Face 4 = 3 (4-3; 4-6; 4-10)
Face 5 = 4 (5-3; 5-6; 5-1; 5-9)
Face 6 = 4 (6-5; 6-7; 6-8; 6-4)
Face 7 = 1 (7-6)
Face 8 = 3 (8-6; 8-9; 8-10)
Face 9 = 3 (9-2; 9-5; 9-8)
Face 10 = 3 (10-2; 10-4; 10-8)

Total = 28

46. Pools
The other five words are palindromes. Palindromes are words or phrases that are spelled the same forward and backward.

47.

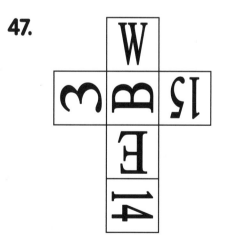

48. They are the same length.

49.
1) 26 letters of the alphabet
2) 1001 Arabian nights
3) 7 Wonders of the World
4) 12 signs of the zodiac
5) 54 cards in a deck (with the jokers)
6) 9 planets in the solar system
7) 88 piano keys
8) 13 stripes on the American flag
9) 32 degrees Fahrenheit at which water freezes
10) 18 holes on a golf course
11) 90 degrees in a right angle
12) 200 dollars for passing go in Monopoly
13) 8 sides on a stop sign
14) 3 blind mice (see how they run)
15) 4 quarts in a gallon
16) 24 hours in a day
17) 1 wheel on a unicycle
18) 5 digits in a zip code
19) 57 Heinz varieties
20) 11 players on a football team
21) 29 days in February in a leap year
22) 64 squares on a checkerboard

50.

R	O	A	S	Y	E	D	B	K
Y	B	K	D	O	R	A	S	E
D	S	E	A	B	K	R	O	Y
O	A	R	E	S	D	K	Y	B
B	K	S	R	A	Y	E	D	O
E	D	Y	B	K	O	S	R	A
A	E	B	Y	D	S	O	K	R
S	Y	O	K	R	A	B	E	D
K	R	D	O	E	B	Y	A	S

51. 11

Add the top two numbers in each circle and divide that sum by five to get the bottom number.

52.

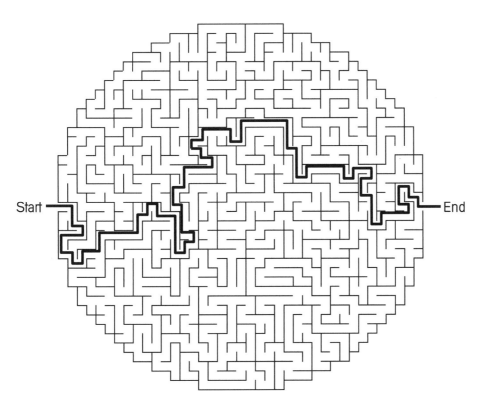

Start — End

53. 8

Add the four corner numbers in each box and divide the sum by four to get the number in the middle.

54. A = 5; B = 4; C = 4; D = 2; E = 2; F = 3; G = 3; H = 4; I = 3; J = 2

55. Aman had the least amount with $0.02.
If Aman and Betsy had $0.12 together and Betsy and Colin had $0.18 together, then Colin had six cents more than Aman. Since Aman and Colin had a total of $0.10 together and Colin had six cents more than Aman, then Colin had $0.08 and Aman had $0.02 (and Betsy had $0.10).

56.

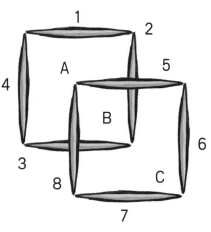

57. Begin at the beginning and go on till you come to the end; then stop.—Lewis Carroll

58.

Egis	His	Swig	Wet
Eight	Hit	The	Wets
Eights	Hits	Thew	Whet
Gest	I	Thews	Whist
Get	Is	This	Whit
Gets	It	Tie	White
Gi	Set	Ties	Whites
Gie	Sew	Twig	Wig
Gies	She	Twigs	Wigs
Gis	Shew	We	Wise
Gist	Sigh	Weigh	Wish
Hegite	Sight	Weighs	Wist
Heist	Sit	Weight	With
Hi	Site	Weights	Wit
Hie	Stew	West	

59. 1) 1:11 uses six segments.
2) 10:08 uses twenty-one segments.

60. L

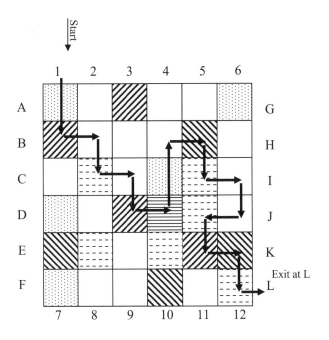

61. They are parallel.

62.

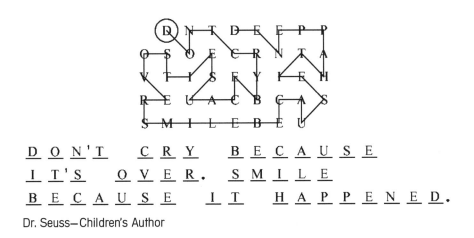

D O N ' T   C R Y   B E C A U S E
I T ' S   O V E R .   S M I L E
B E C A U S E   I T   H A P P E N E D .

Dr. Seuss—Children's Author

63.

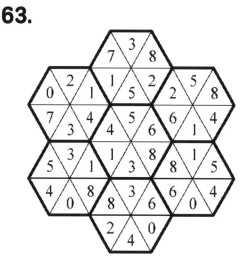

64. Lemons

Take the last three letters of the first word in each set and combine them with the last three letters of the third word. Those six letters will be the word in the middle.

65. A Turn of Events

66. The other state is Tennessee.

For Tennessee, starting from the north and moving clockwise, the adjacent states are:

1) Kentucky

2) Virginia

3) North Carolina

4) Georgia

5) Alabama

6) Mississippi

7) Arkansas

8) Missouri

For Missouri, starting from the north and moving clockwise, the adjacent states are:

1) Iowa

2) Illinois

3) Kentucky

4) Tennessee

5) Arkansas

6) Oklahoma

7) Kansas

8) Nebraska

67.

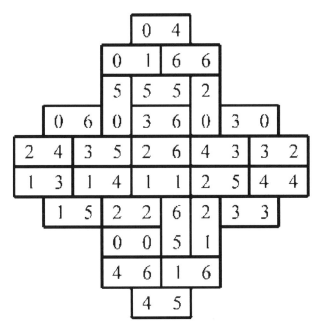

68. Believe it or not, there are no curved lines.

69. Here are twelve answers of the most common parts. Did you find others?

1. Arms
2. Ears
3. Eyes
4. Foot
5. Hair
6. Hand
7. Head
8. Knee
9. Legs
10. Nail
11. Nose
12. Toes

70.

5	2	4	9	3	6	8	7	1
7	8	9	1	2	4	6	3	5
3	6	1	8	7	5	2	4	9
9	7	3	4	5	2	1	6	8
2	1	5	3	6	8	7	9	4
6	4	8	7	1	9	5	2	3
8	5	2	6	4	3	9	1	7
1	3	6	5	9	7	4	8	2
4	9	7	2	8	1	3	5	6

71. It is possible if Sue is Molly's grandmother on her father's side. Let's say Sue had Molly's father, Tim, when she was only twenty years old. Eighteen years later, Tim married Barbara, Molly's mom, who was twelve years older than Tim (12+18 = 30). They had Molly a year later when Barbara was thirty-one and Sue was thirty-nine.

72. Here's one answer with twenty connections:

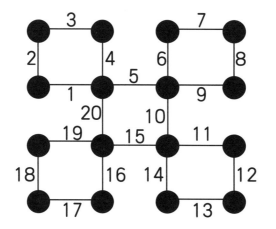

Can you find more than twenty connections?

73. One number: 103

An easy way to start to look for the solution with any number is to start from the back. In other words, start at 107 and count back 4 to 103. The next step is to look for multiples of that number. In this case 103. Since 103 is a prime number, it will have no multiples in the first 100 numbers. Following this formula, no other numbers are prime numbers. So 103 is the only answer.

74.

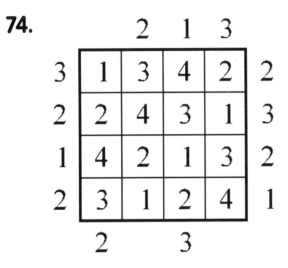

75. They are the same size!

76.

5	4	1	2 < 3
---	---	∧	∧
3	1	2	5	4
	∧	∧	∨
1	2 < 3	4 < 5
4	3	5	1	2
		∧
2	5 > 4	3	1

77. Seventeen times

Did you count the *f* in the word *of*? It also needs to be counted twice in the word *off*.

78. Undercover Detective

79.

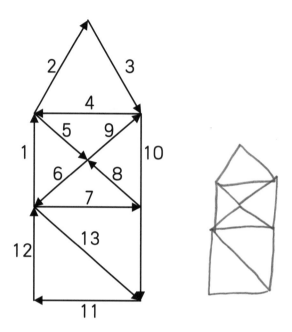

80.

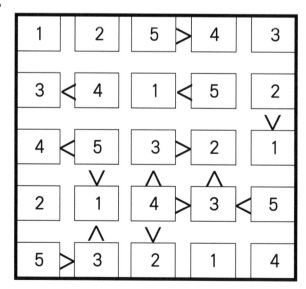

81. T

Working backward, the letter above K is F. Three letters to the right of F is I. Two letters below I is S. And the letter to right of S is T.

82.

Adjectives

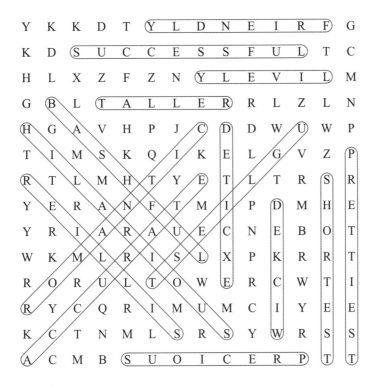

83. Shawna has it. Steve's statement is the only truthful statement. One way to solve this is to assume each statement is true until it proves to be either true or false. If you use this method starting with Pam's statement, the three statements that are false will reveal themselves.

84.

85.

1	2	5	5	1	1
3	5	1	5	4	2
2	1	3	4	5	1
1	5	4	5	2	5
4	5	3	3	1	1
1	4	2	1	3	1

86.

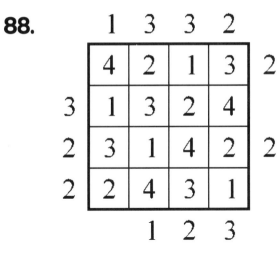

87. She Is Down to Earth

88.

	1	3	3	2	
	4	2	1	3	2
3	1	3	2	4	
2	3	1	4	2	2
2	2	4	3	1	
		1	2	3	

89.

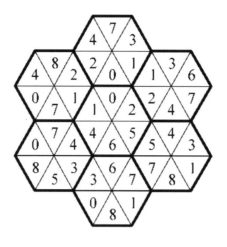

90.

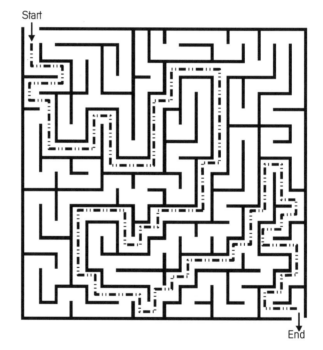